CW00855349

BMP4

Best Management Practices
for Protection against
Somalia Based Piracy

(Version 4 – August 2011)

*Suggested Planning and Operational
Practices for Ship Operators and
Masters of Ships Transiting the
High Risk Area*

Printed August 2011

ISBN: 978 1 85609 505 1

Printed & bound in Great Britain by Bell & Bain Ltd., Glasgow

Published in 2011 by
Witherby Publishing Group Ltd
4 Dunlop Square
Livingston, Edinburgh, EH54 8SB
Scotland, UK

Tel No: +44 (0) 1506 463 227
Fax No: +44 (0) 1506 468 999
Email: info@emailws.com
Web: www.witherbys.com

Contents

The Three Fundamental Requirements of BMP

Register at MSCHOA – Report to UKMTO – Implement SPMs

1. Register at MSCHOA

Ensure that a '**Vessel Movement Registration Form**' has been submitted to MSCHOA prior to entering the High Risk Area (an area bounded by Suez and the Strait of Hormuz to the North, 10°S and 78°E). This may be done directly – online by the Ship's Operator, by fax, or by email. (See Annex E for details of the MSCHOA Vessel Movement Registration Form).

All vessel movements should be registered with MSCHOA even if the vessel is transiting as part of a National Convoy, there is a security team onboard or if not transiting the Gulf of Aden.

2. Report to UKMTO

On entering the UKMTO Voluntary Reporting Area – an area bounded by Suez to the North, 10°S and 78°E - ensure that a UKMTO '**Vessel Position Reporting Form - Initial Report**' is sent (see Annex B).

Vessels are strongly encouraged to report daily to the UKMTO by email at 08:00 hours GMT whilst operating within the High Risk Area. The UKMTO '**Vessel Position Reporting Form - Daily Position Report**' (as set out in Annex B) should be used.

UKMTO acts as the primary point of contact for merchant vessels and liaison with military forces in the region and it is the **primary point of contact** during an attack. For this reason they should be aware that the vessel is transiting the High Risk Area.

3. Implement SPMs

The Ship Protection Measures described in BMP are the most basic that are likely to be effective. Owners may wish to consider making alterations to the vessel beyond the scope of this booklet, and/or provide additional equipment and/or manpower as a means of further reducing the risk of piracy attack.

If pirates are unable to board a ship they cannot hijack it.

Aide Memoire

AVOID BEING A VICTIM OF PIRACY

Do not be ALONE
- Report to UKMTO (email or call) and Register transit with MSCHOA.
- Use the Internationally Recommended Transit Corridor (IRTC) and Group Transit Scheme or Independent Convoy.
- It is recommended to keep AIS turned on.

Do not be DETECTED
- Keep track of NAVWARNS and visit relevant websites (MSCHOA and NATO Shipping Centre) for known pirate operating locations.
- Use navigation lights only.

Do not be SURPRISED
- Increased vigilance - lookouts, CCTV and Radar.

Do not be VULNERABLE
- Use Visible (deterrent) and Physical (preventative) Ship Protection Measures.
- These could include: razor wire, use of water/foam etc.
- Provide additional personal protection to bridge teams.

Do not be BOARDED
- Increase to maximum speed.
- Manoeuvre vessel.

Do not be CONTROLLED
- Follow well practiced procedures and drills.
- Use of Citadels (Only with prior agreement Master/Ship Operator & fully prepared and drilled - Noting a Naval/Military response is not guaranteed.
- Deny use of tools, equipment, access routes.

Introduction

1.1 The purpose of the Industry Best Management Practices (BMP) contained in this booklet is to assist ships to avoid, deter or delay piracy attacks in the High Risk Area, as defined in section 2 (see Page 4). Experience and data collected by Naval/Military forces, shows that the application of the recommendations contained within this booklet can and will make a significant difference in preventing a ship becoming a victim of piracy.

1.2 The potential consequences of not following BMP, as set out in this booklet, are severe. There have been instances of pirates subjecting their hostages to violence and other ill treatment. The average length of a hijacking of vessel and her crew is over 7 months. (Note Naval/Military forces often refer to a 'pirated' vessel rather than a 'hijacked' vessel, but the meaning is the same).

1.3 For the purposes of the BMP the term 'piracy' includes all acts of violence against ships, her crew and cargo. This includes armed robbery and attempts to board and take control of the ship, wherever this may take place. Somali pirates have, to date, sought to hijack a vessel, her cargo and crew and hold them until a ransom demand is paid.

1.4 Where possible, this booklet should be read with reference to the Maritime Security Centre – Horn of Africa (www.MSCHOA.org), and the NATO Shipping Centre, (www.shipping.NATO.int), websites which provide additional regularly updated advice (including up to date alerts on piracy attacks).

1.5 Not all Ship Protection Measures discussed in BMP4 may be applicable to every ship type.

1.6 This BMP4 booklet updates the guidance contained within the 3rd edition of the Best Management Practice document published in June 2010.

1.7 This booklet complements piracy guidance provided in the latest IMO MSC Circulars, see the IMO website at www.imo.org

Nothing in this booklet detracts from the Master's overriding authority to protect his crew, ship and cargo.

Somali Pirate Activity – The High Risk Area

2.1   The presence of Naval/Military forces in the Gulf of Aden, concentrated on the Internationally Recommended Transit Corridor (IRTC), has significantly reduced the incidence of piracy attack in this area. With Naval/Military forces concentrated in this area, Somali pirate activity has been forced out into the Arabian Sea and beyond. It is important to note, however, that there remains a serious and continuing threat from piracy in the Gulf of Aden.

2.2   Somali based pirate attacks have taken place throughout the Gulf of Aden, Arabian Sea and Northern Indian Ocean, affecting all shipping in the region. The recent increasing use of hijacked merchant ships, fishing vessels and dhows as 'Motherships' enables pirates to operate at extreme range from Somalia, carrying attack craft (skiffs) and weapons.

2.3   **Pirate Activity:**

- The level of pirate activity varies within the High Risk Area due to changing weather conditions and activity by Naval/Military forces.

- Pirate activity generally reduces in areas affected by the South West monsoon, and increases in the period following the monsoon.

- The onset of the North East monsoon generally has a lesser effect on piracy activity than the South West monsoon.

- When piracy activity is reduced in one area of the High Risk Area it is likely to increase in another area (eg the area off Kenya and Tanzania, the Gulf of Aden and Bab al-Mandeb all generally experience an increase in pirate activity during the South West monsoon).

2.4 The **High Risk Area** defines itself by where pirate activity and/or attacks have taken place. For the purpose of BMP the High Risk Area is an area bounded by **Suez and the Strait of Hormuz to the North, 10°S and 78°E**. (Note - the UKMTO Voluntary Reporting Area is slightly larger as it includes the Arabian Gulf). **Attacks have taken place at most extremities of the High Risk Area.** Attacks to the South have extended into the Mozambique Channel. A high state of readiness and vigilance should be maintained even to the South of the Southerly limit of the High Risk Area.

2.5 It is important that the latest information on the location of where pirates are operating is used when planning routes through the High Risk Area. It is also important that vessels are prepared to alter course at short notice to avoid pirate activity when information is provided by NAV WARNINGS and/or Naval/Military forces. Weather can also constitute an obstacle to pirates and can be considered a factor when planning a route through the High Risk Area. It is recommended that the latest advice/updates be obtained from MSCHOA, NATO Shipping Centre, and the UKMTO on the extent and latest location of pirate activity. (See contact details at Annex A).

2.6 It is strongly recommended that BMP is applied throughout the High Risk Area.

Risk Assessment

3.1   Prior to transiting the High Risk Area, ship operators and Masters should carry out a thorough Risk Assessment to assess the likelihood and consequences of piracy attacks to the vessel, based on the latest available information (see Annex A for useful contacts, including MSCHOA, NATO Shipping Centre, UKMTO and MARLO). The output of this Risk Assessment should identify measures for prevention, mitigation and recovery, which will mean combining statutory regulations with supplementary measures to combat piracy. It is important that the Risk Assessment is ship and voyage specific, and not generic.

Factors to be considered in the Risk Assessment should include, but may not be limited to, the following:

3.2   **Crew Safety:**

■   The primary consideration should be to ensure the safety of the crew. Care should be taken, when formulating measures to prevent illegal boarding and external access to the accommodation, that crew members will not be trapped inside and should be able to escape in the event of another type of emergency, such as, for example fire.

■   Careful consideration should be given to the location of a Safe Muster Point or Citadel. (See section 8.13).

■   Consideration should also be given to the ballistic protection afforded to the crew who may be required to remain on the bridge during a pirate attack, recognising that pirates increasingly fire at the bridge of a vessel to try to force it to stop. (See section 8.3).

3.3 Freeboard:

■ It is likely that pirates will try to board the ship being attacked at the lowest point above the waterline, making it easier for them to climb onboard. These points are often on either quarter or at the vessel's stern.

■ Experience suggests that vessels with a minimum freeboard that is greater than 8 metres have a much greater chance of successfully escaping a piracy attempt than those with less.

■ A large freeboard will provide little or no protection if the construction of the ship provides access to pirates seeking to climb onboard, and thus further protective measures should be considered.

■ A large freeboard alone may not be enough to deter a pirate attack.

3.4 Speed:

- One of the most effective ways to defeat a pirate attack is by using speed to try to outrun the attackers and/or make it difficult to board.

- To date, there have been no reported attacks where pirates have boarded a ship that has been proceeding at over 18 knots. **It is possible however that pirate tactics and techniques may develop to enable them to board faster moving ships**.

- Ships are recommended to proceed at Full Sea Speed, or at least 18 knots where they are capable of greater speed, throughout their transit of the High Risk Area.

- It is very important to increase to maximum safe speed immediately after identifying any suspicious vessel and as quickly as possible in order to try to open the CPA (Closest Point of Approach) from any possible attackers and/or make the vessel more difficult to board.

- If a vessel is part of a 'Group Transit' (see section 7.9 for further details of Group Transits) within the Internationally Recommended Transit Corridor (IRTC), speed may be required to be adjusted.

- It is recommended that reference should be made to the MSCHOA, NATO Shipping Centre and MARLO websites for the latest threat guidance regarding pirate attack speed capability.

3.5 Sea State:

- Pirates mount their attacks from very small craft (skiffs), even where they are supported by larger vessels or 'Motherships', which tends to limit their operations to moderate sea states.

- It is likely to be more difficult to operate small craft effectively in sea state 3 and above.

8

Typical Pirate Attacks

4.1 Commonly, two small high speed (up to 25 knots) open boats or 'skiffs' are used in attacks, often approaching from either quarter or the stern. Skiffs are frequently fitted with 2 outboard engines or a larger single 60hp engine.

4.2 Pirate Action Groups operate in a number of different boat configurations. To date whatever the configuration the attack phase is carried out by skiffs. Pirate Action Group boat configurations include:

- Skiffs only – usually two.

- Open whalers carrying significant quantities of fuel often towing 2 or more attack skiffs.

- Motherships which have included the very largest of merchant ships, fishing vessels and dhows.

These Motherships have been taken by the pirates and usually have their own crew onboard as hostages. Motherships are used to carry pirates, stores, fuel and attack skiffs to enable pirates to operate over a much larger area and are significantly less affected by the weather. Attack skiffs are often towed

behind the Motherships. Where the size of the Mothership allows it, skiffs are increasingly being carried onboard and camouflaged to reduce chances of interdiction by Naval/ Military forces.

4.3 Increasingly, pirates use small arms fire and Rocket Propelled Grenades (RPGs) in an effort to intimidate Masters of ships to reduce speed and stop to allow the pirates to board. The use of these weapons is generally focused on the bridge and accommodation area. In what are difficult circumstances, it is very important to maintain Full Sea Speed, increasing speed where possible, and using careful manoeuvring to resist the attack.

4.4 Somali pirates seek to place their skiffs alongside the ship being attacked to enable one or more armed pirates to climb onboard. Pirates frequently use long lightweight ladders and ropes, or a long hooked pole with a knotted climbing rope to climb up the side of the vessel being attacked. Once onboard the pirate (or pirates) will generally make their way to the bridge to try to take control of the vessel. Once on the bridge the pirate/pirates will demand that the ship slows/stops to enable further pirates to board.

4.5 Attacks have taken place at most times of the day. However, many pirate attacks have taken place early in the morning, at first light. Attacks have occurred at night, particularly clear moonlit nights, but night time attacks are less common.

4.6 The majority of piracy attacks have been repelled by ship's crew who have planned and trained in advance of the passage and applied the BMPs contained within this booklet.

BMP Reporting Procedures

5.1 An essential part of BMP that applies to all ships is liaison with Naval/Military forces. This is to ensure that Naval/Military forces are aware of the sea passage that a ship is about to embark upon and how vulnerable that ship is to pirate attack. This information is essential to enable the Naval/Military forces to best use the assets available to them. Once ships have commenced their passage it is important that they continue to update the Naval/Military forces on progress. The two key Naval/Military organisations to contact are:

5.1.1 UKMTO:

The UK Maritime Trade Operations (UKMTO) office in Dubai is the first point of contact for ships in the region. The day-to-day interface between Masters and Naval/Military forces is provided by UKMTO, which talks to merchant ships and liaises directly with MSCHOA and Naval Commanders at sea and ashore. Merchant vessels are strongly encouraged to send regular reports to UKMTO.

These comprise:

1. Initial Report,

2. Daily Reports,

3. Final Report (upon departure from the high risk area or arrival in port).

Reporting Forms for use in the UKMTO Voluntary Reporting Area are included at Annex B. UKMTO uses this information to help Naval/Military forces to maintain an accurate picture of merchant shipping (see contact details at Annex A)

5.1.2 MSCHOA:

The Maritime Security Centre – Horn of Africa (MSCHOA) is the planning and coordination centre for EU Naval forces (EUNAVFOR). MSCHOA encourages Companies to register their vessels' movements prior to entering the High Risk Area (including the International Recommended Transit Corridor 'IRTC') via their website (www.mschoa.org). (See contact details at Annex A.) It should be noted that the EUNAVFOR operational area does not extend East of 65°E.

It is important that vessels and their operators complete both the UKMTO Vessel Position Reporting Forms and register with MSCHOA

Operations room UKMTO

Company Planning

Company planning checklist

Company Planning - Prior to entering the High Risk Area		
6.1	**Register ship with MSCHOA website**	It is strongly recommended that ship operators register for access to the restricted sections of the MSCHOA website (www.MSCHOA.org) prior to entering the High Risk Area as it contains additional and updated information. <u>Note that this is not the same as registering a ship's movement - see below.</u>
6.2	**Obtain the latest information from the MSCHOA and NATO Shipping Centre websites**	Great care should be taken in voyage planning in the High Risk Area given that pirate attacks are taking place at extreme range from the Somali Coast. It is important to obtain the latest information from the MSCHOA and NATO Shipping Centre websites (www.MSCHOA.org and www.shipping.NATO.int) before planning and executing a voyage.
6.3	**Review the SSA and SSP**	Review the Ship Security Assessment (SSA) and implementation of the Ship Security Plan (SSP), as required by the International Ship and Port Facility Security Code (ISPS), to counter the piracy threat.
6.4	**Put SSP in place**	The Company Security Officer (CSO) is encouraged to ensure that a SSP is in place for a passage through the High Risk Area, and that this is exercised, briefed and discussed with the Master and the Ship Security Officer (SSO).

6.5	**Monitor piracy related websites on specific threats**	Ensure that ships are aware of any specific threats within the High Risk Areas that have been promulgated on the MSCHOA and NATO Shipping Centre websites – www.mschoa.org and www.shipping.NATO.int. Additionally all NAV WARNINGS – Sat C (NAVTEXT in limited areas) should be monitored and acted upon as appropriate by the ship's Master.
6.6	**Offer guidance to Master with regard to the recommended route**	Offer the ship's Master guidance with regard to the recommended routeing through the High Risk Area and details of the piracy threat. Guidance should be provided on the available methods of transiting the IRTC, (eg a Group Transit or National Convoys where these exist). ■ Group Transits coordinated by MSCHOA within the IRTC, group vessels together by speed for maximum protection. Further details of Group Transit schemes including departure timings can be found on the MSCHOA website. ■ National Convoys. A number of Naval/Military forces offer protected convoys through the IRTC. Details of the convoy schedules may be found on the MSCHOA website.

6.7	**Plan and install Ship Protection Measures**	The provision of carefully planned and installed Ship Protection Measures prior to transiting the High Risk Area is very strongly recommended. Suggested Ship Protection Measures are set out within this booklet – see section 8. It has been proven that the use of Ship Protection Measures significantly increases the prospects of a ship resisting a pirate attack.
6.8	**Conduct crew training**	Conduct crew training sessions (including Citadel Drills where utilised) prior to transits and debriefing sessions post transits.
Company Planning - Upon entering the High Risk Area		
6.9	**Submit 'Vessel Movement Registration Form' to MSCHOA**	Ensure that a 'Vessel Movement Registration Form' has been submitted to MSCHOA. This may be done directly – online by the ship's operator, by fax, or by email. (See Annex E for details of the MSCHOA Vessel Movement Registration Form.

Be aware that UKMTO is unable to respond as an SSAS designated recipient when a vessel is outside the UKMTO Voluntary Reporting Area.

The ship operator should ensure that BMP measures are in place prior to entry into the High Risk Area

16

Ship Master's Planning

Ship Master's Planning - Prior to entering the High Risk Area		
7.1	**Brief crew and conduct drill**	Prior to entry into the High Risk Area it is recommended that the crew should be fully briefed on the preparations and a drill conducted. The plan should be reviewed and all personnel briefed on their duties, including familiarity with the alarm signifying a piracy attack, an all clear and the appropriate response to each. The drill should also consider the following: ■ Testing the vessel's Ship Protection Measures, including testing of the security of all access points. ■ The Ship Security Plan should be thoroughly reviewed (see section 6.4).
7.2	**Prepare an Emergency Communication Plan**	Masters are advised to prepare an Emergency Communication Plan, to include all essential emergency contact numbers and prepared messages, which should be ready at hand or permanently displayed near all external communications stations (eg telephone numbers of the UKMTO, MSCHOA, Company Security Officer etc – see list of Contacts at Annex A).

7.3	Define the ship's AIS policy	Although the Master has the discretion to switch off the AIS if he believes that its use increases the ship's vulnerability, in order to provide Naval/Military forces with tracking information it is recommended that AIS is left on throughout the High Risk Area, but that it is restricted to ship's identity, position, course, speed, navigational status and safety-related information. The recommendation to keep the AIS on will be the subject of ongoing review - any updates will be notified on the MSCHOA and NATO Shipping Centre websites.
7.4	If Company has not submitted 'Vessel Movement Registration Form' to MSCHOA	Ensure MSCHOA 'Vessel Movement Registration Form' has been completed and submitted by the Company. If the Form has not been submitted by the Company the Master should submit it by email / fax.
Masters' Planning - Upon entering the High Risk Area		
7.5	Upon entering submit 'Vessel Position Reporting Form'-Initial Report to UKMTO	On entering the UKMTO Voluntary Reporting Area - an area bounded by Suez to the North, 10°S and 78°E - ensure that a UKMTO 'Vessel Position Reporting Form' - Initial Report is sent (see Annex B).

The Master should ensure that BMP measures are in place prior to entry into the High Risk Area

Transiting through the High Risk Area		
7.6	**Reduce maintenance and engineering work to minimum**	Maintenance and engineering work in the High Risk Area – The following is recommended: ■ Any work outside of the accommodation is strictly controlled and similarly access points limited and controlled. ■ All Engine Room essential equipment is immediately available – no maintenance on essential equipment.
7.7	**Daily submit 'Vessel Position Reporting Form - Daily Position Report' to UKMTO**	Vessels are strongly encouraged to report daily to the UKMTO by email at 08:00 hours GMT whilst operating within the High Risk Area. The UKMTO 'Vessel Position Reporting Form - Daily Position Report' (as set out in Annex B) should be used.
7.8	**Carefully review all warnings and information**	The Master (and Company) should appreciate that the voyage routeing may need to be reviewed in light of updated information received. This information and warnings may be provided by a number of different means including NAV WARNINGS – Sat C (and NAVTEXT in limited areas). It is important that all warnings and information are carefully reviewed.

Prior to entering the International Recommended Transit Corridor (IRTC)		
7.9	**Use IRTC 'Group Transit Scheme' while transiting through Gulf of Aden**	It is strongly recommended that ships navigate within the IRTC, where Naval/Military forces are concentrated. Naval/Military forces operate the 'Group Transit Scheme' within the IRTC which is coordinated by MSCHOA. This scheme groups vessels together by speed for maximum protection for their transit through the IRTC. Further guidance on the 'Group Transit Scheme', including the departure timings for the different groups, is included on the MSCHOA website or can be obtained by fax from MSCHOA (see contact details at Annex A). Use of the 'Group Transit Scheme' is recommended. Masters should note that warships might not be within visual range of the ships in the 'Group Transit Scheme', but this does not lessen the protection afforded by the scheme.
7.10	**Make adjustments to passage plans to conform to MSCHOA advice.**	Ships may be asked to make adjustments to passage plans to conform to MSCHOA advice. Ships joining a Group Transit should: ■ Carefully time their arrival to avoid a slow speed approach to the forming up point (Point A or B).

		■ Avoid waiting at the forming up point (Point A or B). ■ Note that ships are particularly vulnerable to a pirate attack if they slowly approach or wait at the forming up points (Points A and B).
7.11	**National Convoys**	Some countries offer independent convoy escorts through the IRTC where merchant vessels are escorted by a warship. Details of the convoy schedules and how to apply to be included are detailed on the MSCHOA website (www. mschoa.org). It should be noted that most national convoys require prior registration to enable vessels to join the convoy. Ships joining national convoys should note the issues in the bullet points 7.10 as they are also highly relevant to vessels timing their arrival at a national convoy forming up point.

Ships should avoid entering Yemeni territorial waters (12 miles) while on transit as it is very difficult for international Naval/Military forces (non-Yemeni) to protect ships that are attacked inside Yemeni territorial waters.

Ship Protection Measures

8.1 Introduction

The guidance within this section primarily focuses on preparations that might be within the capability of the ship's crew, or with some external assistance.

The guidance is based on experience of piracy attacks to date and may require amendment over time if the pirates change their methods.

The Ship Protection Measures described in BMP are the most basic that are likely to be effective. Owners may wish to consider making further alterations to the vessel beyond the scope of this booklet, and/or provide additional equipment and/or manpower as a means of further reducing the risk of piracy attack. If pirates are unable to board a ship they cannot hijack it.

8.2 Watchkeeping and Enhanced Vigilance

Prior to entering the High Risk Area, it is recommended that preparations are made to support the requirement for increased vigilance by:

- Providing additional lookouts for each Watch. Additional lookouts should be fully briefed.

- Considering a shorter rotation of the Watch period in order to maximise alertness of the lookouts.

- Ensuring that there are sufficient binoculars for the enhanced Bridge Team, preferably anti glare.

- Considering use of night vision optics.

- Maintaining a careful Radar Watch.

Well constructed dummies placed at strategic locations around the vessel can give an impression of greater numbers of people on watch.

A proper lookout is the single most effective method of ship protection where early warning of a suspicious approach or attack is assured, and where defences can be readily deployed

8.3 Enhanced Bridge Protection

The bridge is usually the focus for any pirate attack. In the initial part of the attack, pirates direct weapons fire at the bridge to try to coerce the ship to stop. If they are able to board the vessel the pirates usually try to make for the bridge to enable them to take control. The following further protection enhancements might be considered:

- Kevlar jackets and helmets available for the bridge team to provide a level of protection for those on the bridge during an attack. (If possible, jackets and helmets should be in a non-military colour).

- While most bridge windows are laminated, further protection against flying glass can be provided by the application of security glass film, often called Blast Resistant Film.

- Fabricated metal, (steel/aluminium), plates for the side and rear bridge windows and the bridge wing door windows, which may be rapidly secured in place in the event of an attack.

- The after part of both bridge wings, (often open), can be protected by a wall of sandbags.

- The sides and rear of the bridge, and the bridge wings, may be protected with a double layer of chain link fence which has been shown to reduce the effect of an RPG round. Proprietary anti-RPG screens are also available.

8.4   Control of Access to Bridge, Accommodation and Machinery Spaces

It is very important to control access routes to deter or delay pirates who have managed to board a vessel and are trying to enter accommodation or machinery spaces. It is very important to recognise that if pirates do gain access to the upper deck of a vessel they will be tenacious in their efforts to gain access to the accommodation section and in particular the bridge. It is strongly recommended that significant effort is expended prior to entry to the High Risk Area to deny the pirates access to the accommodation and the bridge.

- All doors and hatches providing access to the bridge, accommodation and machinery spaces should be properly secured to prevent them being opened by pirates.

- Careful consideration should be given to the means of securing doors and hatches in order to afford the ship the maximum protection possible.

- Where the door or hatch is located on an escape route from a manned compartment, it is essential that it can be opened by a seafarer trying to exit by that route. Where the door or hatch is locked it is essential that a key is available, in a clearly visible position by the door or hatch.

- It is recommended that once doors and hatches are secured, a designated and limited number are used for routine access when required, their use being strictly controlled by the Officer of the Watch.

- Consideration should be given to blocking or lifting external ladders on the accommodation block to prevent their use, and to restrict external access to the bridge.

- Where doors and hatches are required to be closed for watertight integrity, ensure all clips are fully dogged down in addition to any locks. Where possible, additional securing such as with wire strops may enhance hatch security.

- Pirates have been known to gain access through portholes and windows. The fitting of steel bars to windows will prevent this even if they manage to shatter the window.

- Prior to entering the High Risk Area procedures for controlling access to accommodation, machinery spaces and store rooms should be set out and practised.

8.5 Physical Barriers

Pirates typically use long lightweight hooked ladders, grappling hooks with rope attached and long hooked poles with a climbing rope attached to board vessels underway. Physical barriers should be used to make it as difficult as possible to gain access to vessels by increasing the height and difficulty of any climb for an attacking pirate.

> **Before constructing any physical barriers it is recommended that a thorough survey is conducted to identify areas vulnerable to pirates trying to gain access.**

■ Razor Wire

Razor wire (also known as barbed tape) creates an effective barrier but only when carefully deployed. The barbs on the wire are designed to have a piercing and gripping action. Care should be taken when selecting appropriate razor wire as the quality (wire gauge and frequency of barbs) and type will vary considerably. Lower quality razor wire is unlikely to be effective. Three main types of razor wire are commonly available:

♦ Unclipped (straight strand),

♦ Spiral (like a telephone cord) and

♦ Concertina (linked spirals).

Concertina razor wire is recommended as the linked spirals make it the most effective barrier. Razor wire should be constructed of high tensile wire, which is difficult to cut with hand tools. Concertina razor wire coil diameters of approximately 730 mm or 980 mm are recommended.

When deploying razor wire personal protective equipment to protect hands, arms and faces must be used. Moving razor wire using wire hooks (like meat hooks) rather than by gloved hand reduces the risk of injury. It is recommended that razor wire is provided in shorter sections (e.g. 10 metre section) as it is significantly easier and safer to use than larger sections which can be very heavy and unwieldy.

A robust razor wire barrier is particularly effective if it is:

- ◆ Constructed outboard of the ship's structure (i.e. overhanging) to make it more difficult for pirates to hook on their boarding ladder/grappling hooks to the ship's structure.

- ◆ Constructed of a double roll of concertina wire - some vessels use a treble roll of concertina razor wire which is even more effective.

- ◆ Properly secured to the vessel to prevent pirates pulling off the razor wire, with for example the hook of a boarding ladder. Consideration should also be given to further securing the razor wire with a wire strop through the razor wire to prevent it being dislodged.

- ■ Some vessels utilise fixed metal grilles topped with metal spikes as an effective barrier.

- Electrified barriers are not recommended for hydrocarbon carrying vessels but, following a full risk assessment, can be appropriate and effective for some other types of vessel.

- It is recommended that warning signs of the electrified fence or barrier are displayed - inward facing in English/language of the crew, outward facing in Somali.

- The use of such outward facing warning signs might also be considered as a deterrent even if no part of the barrier is actually electrified.

KHATAR

Deyr Danab Koronto Sare (Xooggan)

*Example of a warning sign in Somali, which states –
DANGER HIGH VOLTAGE ELECTRIC BARRIER*

Picture courtesy of NATO

8.6   Water Spray and Foam Monitors

The use of water spray and/or foam monitors has been found to be effective in deterring or delaying pirates attempting to board a vessel. The use of water can make it difficult for a pirate skiff to remain alongside and makes it significantly more difficult for a pirate to try to climb onboard. Options include:

■   Fire hoses and foam monitors – Manual operation of hoses and foam monitors is not recommended as this is likely to place the operator in a particularly exposed position and therefore it is recommended that hoses and foam monitors (delivering water) should be fixed in position to cover likely pirate access routes. Improved water coverage may be achieved by using fire hoses in jet mode but by utilising baffle plates fixed a short distance in front of the nozzle.

■   Water cannons – These are designed to deliver water in a vertical sweeping arc thus protecting a greater part of the hull. Many of these have been developed from tank cleaning machines.

■   Ballast pumps – Where possible to do so ships may utilise their ballast pumps to flood the deck with water thus providing a highly effective water curtain over the ship's side. This may be achieved by allowing ballast tanks to over-flow on to the deck, by using existing pipework when in ballast condition, or by retrofitting pipework to allow flooding of the decks whilst in loaded condition. Care must be taken to ensure that ballast tanks are not over-pressurised causing damage to the hull and tanks, or vessel stability compromised. If in doubt it is recommended that the relevant Classification Society be contacted for advice.

■ Steam – Hot water, or using a diffuser nozzle to produce steam has also been found to be very effective in deterring attacks.

■ Water spray rails - Some ships have installed spray rails using a Glass Reinforced Plastic (GRP) water main, with spray nozzles to produce a water curtain to cover larger areas.

■ Foam can be used, but it must be in addition to a vessel's standard Fire Fighting Equipment (FFE) stock. Foam is effective as it is disorientating and very slippery making it difficult to climb through.

The following points are also worthy of note:

- Once rigged and fixed in position it is recommended that hoses and foam monitors are in a ready state, requiring just the remote activation of fire pumps to commence delivery of water.

- Where possible no maintenance should be carried out on the vessel's sea water systems whilst on passage in the High Risk Area. Note that in order to utilise all pumps additional power may be required and therefore these systems should also be ready for immediate use.

- Practice, observation, and drills will be required in order to ensure that the results achieved by the equipment, provide effective coverage of vulnerable areas.

8.7 Alarms

Sounding the ship's alarms/whistle serves to inform the vessel's crew that a piracy attack has commenced and, importantly, demonstrates to any potential attacker that the ship is aware of the attack and is reacting to it. If approached, continuous sounding of the vessel's foghorn/whistle distracts the pirates and as above lets them know that they have been seen. It is important to ensure that:

- The piracy alarm is distinctive to avoid confusion with other alarms, potentially leading to the crew mustering at the wrong location outside the accommodation.

- Crew members are familiar with each alarm, including the signal warning of an attack and an all clear, and the appropriate response to it.

- Exercises are carried out prior to entering the High Risk Area.

8.8 Manoeuvring Practice

Practising manoeuvring the vessel prior to entry into the High Risk Area will be very beneficial and will ensure familiarity with the ship's handling characteristics and how to effect anti-piracy manoeuvres whilst maintaining the best possible speed. (Waiting until the ship is attacked before practising this is too late!)

> **Where navigationally safe to do so, Masters are encouraged to practise manoeuvring their ships to establish which series of helm orders produce the most difficult sea conditions for pirate skiffs trying to attack, without causing a significant reduction in the ship's speed.**

8.9   Closed Circuit Television (CCTV)

Once an attack is underway and pirates are firing weaponry at the vessel, it is difficult and dangerous to observe whether the pirates have managed to gain access. The use of CCTV coverage allows a degree of monitoring of the progress of the attack from a less exposed position:

- Consider the use of CCTV cameras to ensure coverage of vulnerable areas, particularly the poop deck.
- Consider positioning CCTV monitors at the rear of the bridge in a protected position.
- Further CCTV monitors could be located at the Safe Muster Point/Citadel (see section 8.13)
- Recorded CCTV footage may provide useful evidence after an attack.

8.10 Upper Deck Lighting

It is recommended that the following lights are available and tested:

- Weather deck lighting around the accommodation block and rear facing lighting on the poop deck, consistent with Rule 20(b) of the International Regulations for Preventing Collision at Sea.
- Search lights for immediate use when required.
- It is, however, recommended that ships proceed with just their navigation lights illuminated, with the lighting described above extinguished. Once pirates have been identified or an attack commences, illuminating the lighting described above demonstrates to the pirates that they have been observed.
- Navigation lights should not be switched off at night.

8.11 Deny Use of Ship's Tools and Equipment

Pirates generally board vessels with little in the way of equipment other than personal weaponry. It is important to try to deny pirates the use of ship's tools or equipment that may be used to gain entry into the vessel. Tools and equipment that may be of use to the pirates should be stored in a secure location.

8.12 Protection of Equipment Stored on the Upper Deck

Small arms and other weaponry are often directed at the vessel and are particularly concentrated on the bridge, accommodation section and poop deck.

- Consideration should be given to providing protection, in the form of sandbags or Kevlar blankets, to gas bottles (i.e. oxy-acetylene) or containers of flammable liquids that must be stored in these locations.
- Ensure that any excess gas bottles or flammable materials are landed prior to transit.

8.13 Safe Muster Points / Citadels

Any decision to navigate in waters where the vessel's security may be threatened requires careful consideration and detailed planning to ensure the safety of the crew and vessel. Consideration should be given to establishing a Safe Muster Point or secure Citadel and an explanation of each follows:

Safe Muster Point:

- A Safe Muster Point is a designated area chosen to provide maximum physical protection to the crew, preferably low down within the vessel.

- In the event of a suspicious approach, members of the crew not required on the Bridge or the Engine Room Control Room will muster.

- A Safe Muster Point is a short-term safe haven, which will provide ballistic protection should the pirates commence firing with small arms weaponry or RPGs.

Citadels:

If Citadels are to be employed, they should be complementary to, rather than a replacement for, all other Ship Protection Measures set out in BMP4. **The establishing of a Citadel may be beyond the capability of ship's staff alone, and may well require external technical advice and support**.

A Citadel is a designated pre-planned area purpose built into the ship where, in the event of imminent boarding by pirates, all crew will seek protection. A Citadel is designed and constructed to resist a determined pirate trying to gain entry for a fixed period of time. The details of the construction and operation of Citadels are beyond the scope of this booklet. A detailed document containing guidance and advice is included on the MSCHOA and NATO Shipping Centre website.

The whole concept of the Citadel approach is lost if any crew member is left outside before it is secured.

Ship operators and Masters are strongly advised to check the MSCHOA website for detailed up to date advice and guidance regarding the construction and operation of Citadels including the criteria that Naval/Military forces will apply before considering a boarding operation to release the crew from the Citadel. (see contact details in Annex A).

- It is important to note that Naval/Military forces will apply the following criteria before a boarding to release those in a Citadel can be considered:

  ♦ 100% of the crew must be secured in the Citadel.

  ♦ The crew of the ship must have self contained, independent, reliable 2-way external communications (sole reliance on VHF communications is <u>not</u> sufficient).

  ♦ The pirates must be denied access to ship propulsion.

- **The use of a Citadel, even where the above criteria are applied, cannot guarantee a Naval/Military response.**

8.14 Unarmed Private Maritime Security Contractors

The use of unarmed Private Maritime Security Contractors is a matter for individual ship operators following their own voyage risk assessment. The deployment onboard is subject to the national laws of the Flag State. The use of experienced and competent unarmed Private Maritime Security Contractors can be a valuable addition to BMP.

8.15 Armed Private Maritime Security Contractors

The use, or not, of armed Private Maritime Security Contractors onboard merchant vessels is a matter for individual ship operators to decide following their own voyage risk assessment and approval of respective Flag States. This advice does not constitute a recommendation or an endorsement of the general use of armed Private Maritime Security Contractors.

Subject to risk analysis, careful planning and agreements the provision of Military Vessel Protection Detachments (VPDs) deployed to protect vulnerable shipping is the recommended option when considering armed guards.

If armed Private Maritime Security Contractors are to be used they must be as an additional layer of protection and not as an alternative to BMP.

If armed Private Maritime Security Contractors are present on board a merchant vessel, this fact should be included in reports to UKMTO and MSCHOA.

The International Maritime Organization (IMO) have produced guidance in the form of IMO Circulars for ship operators and Masters and for Flag States on the use of Private Maritime Security Contractors on board ships in the High Risk Area.

The current IMO Guidance on the use of armed Private Maritime Security Contractors is included on the MSCHOA website. (www.mschoa.org).

Pirate Attack

9.1 If the crew of a vessel suspects that it is coming under a pirate attack there are specific actions that are recommended to be taken during the approach stage and the attack stage. It should be noted that the pirates generally do not use weapons until they are within two cables of a vessel, therefore any period up until this stage can be considered as 'approach', and gives a vessel valuable time in which to activate her defences and make it clear to pirates that they have been seen and the vessel is prepared and will resist.

9.2 Approach Stage

■ If not already at full speed, increase to maximum to open the CPA. Try to steer a straight course to maintain a maximum speed.

■ Initiate the ship's pre-prepared emergency procedures.

■ Activate the Emergency Communication Plan

♦ Sound the emergency alarm and make a 'Pirate Attack' announcement in accordance with the Ship's Emergency Plan

♦ Report the attack immediately to UKMTO (+971 505 523 215). UKMTO is the primary point of contact during an attack but MSCHOA acts as a back-up contact point. Once established, maintain communication with UKMTO. Please report attack to UKMTO even if part of a national convoy so other merchant ships can be warned.

♦ Activate the Ship Security Alert System (SSAS), which will alert your Company Security Officer and Flag State. Make a 'Mayday' call on VHF Ch. 16 (and backup Ch. 08, which is monitored by naval units).

♦ Send a distress message via the Digital Selective Calling system (DSC) and Inmarsat-C, as applicable.

♦ Ensure that the Automatic Identification System (AIS) is switched ON.

■ All crew, except those required on the bridge or in the engine room, should muster at the Safe Muster Point or Citadel if constructed, so that the crew are given as much ballistic protection as possible should the pirates get close enough to use weapons.

■ Where possible, alter course away from the approaching skiffs and/or Motherships. When sea conditions allow, consider altering course to increase an approaching skiff's exposure to wind/waves.

■ Activate water spray and other appropriate self-defensive measures.

■ Ensure that all external doors and, where possible, internal public rooms and cabins, are fully secured.

■ In addition to the emergency alarms and announcements for the benefit of the vessel's crew sound the ship's whistle/foghorn continuously to demonstrate to any potential attacker that the ship is aware of the attack and is reacting to it.

9.3 Attack stage

■ Reconfirm that all ship's personnel are in a position of safety.

■ As the pirates close in on the vessel, Masters should commence small alterations of helm whilst maintaining speed to deter skiffs from lying alongside the vessel in preparation for a boarding attempt. These manoeuvres will create additional wash to impede the operation of the skiffs.

■ Substantial amounts of helm are not recommended, as these are likely to significantly reduce a vessel's speed.

If the Pirates take Control

10.1 Try to remain calm.

10.2 Before the pirates gain access to the bridge, inform UKMTO. Ensure that the SSAS has been activated, and ensure that the AIS is switched on.

10.3 Offer no resistance to the pirates once they reach the bridge. Once on the bridge the pirates are likely to be aggressive, highly agitated, and possibly under the influence of drugs (including khat, an amphetamine like stimulant), so remaining calm and cooperating fully will greatly reduce the risk of harm.

10.4 If the bridge/engine room is to be evacuated the main engine should be stopped and all way taken off the vessel if possible (and if navigationally safe to do so). All remaining crew members should proceed to the designated Safe Muster Point with their hands visible.

10.5 Leave any CCTV running.

In the Event of Military Action

11.1 In the event that Naval/Military forces take action onboard the ship, all personnel should keep low to the deck and cover their head with both hands, with hands visible. On no account should personnel make movements which could be misinterpreted as being aggressive.

11.2 Do not use flash photography.

11.3 Be prepared to be challenged on your identity. Brief and prepare ship's personnel to expect this and to cooperate fully during any Naval/Military action onboard.

11.4 Be aware that English is not the working language of all Naval/Military forces in the region.

Naval/Military forces will endeavour to respond rapidly to ongoing acts of piracy. However because of the very large distances across the High Risk Area a Naval/Military response may not be possible.

Post Incident Reporting

12.1 Following any piracy attack or suspicious activity, it is vital that a detailed report of the event (as per Annex D of this booklet), is provided to UKMTO and MSCHOA. It is also helpful to provide a copy of the report to the IMB. It is important that the report contains descriptions and distinguishing features of any suspicious vessels that were observed. This will ensure full analysis and trends in piracy activity are established and will enable assessment of piracy techniques or changes in tactics, in addition to ensuring appropriate warnings can be issued to other merchant shipping in the vicinity.

12.2 Masters are, therefore, requested to complete the standardised piracy report form contained in Annex D.

12.3 Note that ship operators may also be required to forward a copy of the completed standardised piracy attack report (contained in Annex D) to their Flag State, and in any event are encouraged to do so.

Prosecution of Pirates - Assisting Law Enforcement Authorities

12.4 For Naval/Military forces to hold suspected pirates, following a piracy incident, a witness statement from those affected by the piracy incident is required. Seafarers are encouraged to provide witness statements to Naval/Military forces or law enforcement officers as appropriate when requested to do so to enable suspected pirates to be held and handed over to prosecuting States. Without supporting evidence, including witness statements from those affected by the piracy incident, suspected pirates are unlikely to be prosecuted.

12.5 Law enforcement authorities will routinely request permission to conduct post-release crew debriefs and to collect evidence for ongoing and future investigations and prosecutions following captivity. A thorough investigation is critical to ensure that potential physical evidence, including electronic evidence, is not tainted or destroyed or potential witnesses overlooked. The company and crew are advised that the quality of evidence provided and the availability of the crew to testify will significantly help any investigation or prosecution that follows.

12.6 INTERPOL is an international police organisation with 188 member countries which facilitates cross border police co-operation to combat international crime.

12.7 INTERPOL has a secure website to provide support to ship operators who have had their vessels hijacked by pirates. INTERPOL recognises that seafarers as the victims of piracy must be dealt with in a sympathetic and professional manner. INTERPOL's Maritime Piracy Task Force can assist in taking the appropriate steps to preserve the integrity of the evidence left behind at the crime scene. INTERPOL has a Command and Co-ordination Centre (CCC) which supports any of the 188 member countries faced with a crisis situation or requiring urgent operational assistance. The CCC operates in all four of INTERPOL's official languages (English, French, Spanish and Arabic) and is staffed 24 hours a day, 365 days a year. It is recommended that ship operators contact INTERPOL within 3 days of a hijacking of their vessel.

12.8 INTERPOL may be consulted to discuss the recommended best practices and protocols for the preservation of evidence or other physical clues that could be useful to law enforcement agents pursuing an investigation of the incident. The 24hr telephone contact details for the CCC and INTERPOL's Maritime Task Force website are contained in Annex A and set out below:

CCC 24hr telephone helpline: +33(0) 4 72 44 76 76
Website: www.interpol.int

Updating Best Management Practices

13.1 The Industry Organisations engaged in producing this Booklet will endeavour to meet regularly and will ensure the BMPs are updated as necessary, based upon operational experience and lessons learned.

13.2 The latest advice may be found on the MSCHOA, NATO Shipping Centre and MARLO websites. Additionally the UKMTO may be contacted at any time for updated advice.

Useful Contact Details

1) UKMTO

- Email: UKMTO@eim.ae
- Telephone (24hrs): +971 50 552 3215

2) MSCHOA

- Via Website
  for reporting: www.mschoa.org
- Email: postmaster@mschoa.org
- Telephone: +44 (0) 1923 958545
- Fax: +44 (0) 1923 958520

3) NATO SHIPPING CENTRE

- Website: www.shipping.nato.int
- Email: info@shipping.nato.int
- Telephone (24hrs): +44(0)1923 956574
- Fax: +44(0)1923 956575

4) MARLO

- Website: www.cusnc.navy.mil/marlo/
- Email: marlo.bahrain@me.navy.mil
- Office: +973 1785 3925
- Duty (24hrs): +973 3940 1395
- Fax : +973 1785 3930

5) INTERPOL

- Website: www.interpol.int
- Email: os-ccc@interpol.int
- Telephone (24hrs): +33(0) 4 72 44 76 76

6) IMB

- Email: piracy@icc-ccs.org
- Telephone: +60 3 2031 0014
- Fax: +60 3 2078 5769
- Telex: MA34199 IMBPC1

UKMTO Vessel Position Reporting Forms

Once a vessel has transmitted an Initial Report to UKMTO, then UKMTO will reply and request Daily Reports to be transmitted. Upon reaching port, or upon exiting the High Risk Area, UKMTO will request a Final Report to be transmitted. The following forms are provided:

- Initial Report Format
- Daily Report Format
- Final Report Format.

Masters and Owners should check with the MSCHOA website for the latest information regarding the UKMTO Voluntary Reporting Area (www.MSCHOA.org) or directly with UKMTO (+971 505 523 215).

UKMTO Vessel Position Reporting Form - Initial Report

01	Ship Name	
02	Flag	
03	IMO Number	
04	INMARSAT Telephone Number	
05	Time & Position	
06	Course	
07	Passage Speed	
08	Freeboard	
09	Cargo	
10	Destination and Estimated Time of Arrival	

11	Name and contact details of Company Security Officer	
12	Nationality of Master and Crew	
13	Armed/unarmed security team embarked	

UKMTO Vessel Position Reporting Form - Daily Position Report

01	Ship's name	
02	Ship's Call Sign and IMO Number	
03	Time of Report in UTC	
04	Ship's Position	
05	Ship's Course and Speed	
06	Any other important information	
07	ETA point A/B IRTC (if applicable)	

The other important information could be change of destination or ETA, number of UK personnel on board etc.

UKMTO Vessel Position Reporting Form - Final Report

01	Ship's name	
02	Ship's Call Sign and IMO Number	
03	Time of Report in UTC	
04	Port or position when leaving the voluntary reporting area	

Piracy Definitions

1. It is important to use common definitions and guidelines when reporting piracy attacks and suspicious activity because this will ensure:

    ■ Harmonised data assessment.

    ■ Provision of consistent reporting.

    ■ Harmonised intelligence gathering.

2. 'Piracy' is defined in the 1982 United Nations Convention on the Law of the Sea (UNCLOS) (article 101). However, for the purposes of these BMP, it is important to provide clear, practical, working guidance to the Industry to enable accurate and consistent assessment of suspicious activity and piracy attacks.

3. The following are the BMP Guidelines to assist in assessing what is a piracy attack and what is suspicious activity:

    ■ A piracy attack may include, (but is not limited to), actions such as the following:

        ◆ The use of violence against the ship or its personnel, or any attempt to use violence.

        ◆ Attempt(s) to board the vessel where the Master suspects the persons are pirates.

        ◆ An actual boarding whether successful in gaining control of the vessel or not.

        ◆ Attempts to overcome the Ship Protection Measures by the use of:

- o Ladders.
- o Grappling hooks.
- o Weapons deliberately used against or at the vessel.
- For the purposes of BMP the following definitions distinguish between the differing levels of pirate activity:

Pirate Attack

A piracy attack as opposed to an approach is where a vessel has been subjected to an aggressive approach by a pirate craft AND weapons have been discharged.

Hijack

A hijack is where pirates have boarded and taken control of a vessel against the crew's will.

Illegal Boarding

An illegal boarding is where pirates have boarded a vessel but HAVE NOT taken control. Command remains with the Master. The most obvious example of this is the Citadel scenario.

Suspicious or Aggressive Approach

4. Guidelines for defining suspicious activity:

- Action taken by another craft may be deemed suspicious if any of the following occur (the list is not exhaustive):
  - ◆ A definite course alteration towards the craft associated with a rapid increase in speed, by the suspected craft, that cannot be accounted for as normal activity in the circumstances prevailing in the area.

- Small craft sailing on the same course and speed for an uncommon period and distance, not in keeping with normal fishing or other circumstances prevailing in the area.

- Sudden changes in course towards the vessel and aggressive behaviour.

5. Guidance Note:

- In helping to evaluate suspicious activity, the following may be of assistance to determine the nature of a suspect vessel:

    1. The number of crew on board relative to its size.

    2. The Closest Point of Approach (CPA).

    3. The existence of unusual and non-fishing equipment, e.g. ladders, climbing hooks or large amounts of fuel onboard.

    4. If the craft is armed in excess of the level commonly experienced in the area.

    5. If weapons are fired in the air.

- This is not an exhaustive listing. Other events, activity and craft may be deemed suspicious by the Master of a merchant vessel having due regard to their own seagoing experiences within the High Risk Area and information shared amongst the international maritime community. The examples above are to be treated only as guidance and are not definitive or exhaustive.

Follow-up Report

Following any piracy attack or suspicious activity, it is vital that a detailed report of the event is provided to UKMTO and MSCHOA. It is also helpful to provide a copy of the report to the IMB.

PIRACY ATTACK REPORT VESSEL PARTICULARS/DETAILS:

General Details

01	Name of Ship:
02	IMO No:
03	Flag:
04	Call Sign:
05	Type of Ship:
06	Tonnages: GRT: NRT: DWT:
07	Owner's (Address & Contact Details):
08	Manager's (Address & Contact Details):
09	Last Port/Next Port:
10	Cargo Details: (Type/Quantity)

Details of Incident

11	Date & Time of Incident: LT UTC
12	Position: Lat: (N/S) Long: (E/W)
13	Nearest Land Mark/Location:
14	Port/Town/Anchorage Area:
15	Country/Nearest Country:
16	Status (Berth/Anchored/Steaming):
17	Own Ship's Speed:
18	Ship's Freeboard During Attack:
19	Weather During Attack (Rain/Fog/Mist/Clear/etc, Wind (Speed and Direction), Sea/Swell Height):
20	Types of Attack (Boarded/Attempted):
21	Consequences for Crew, Ship and Cargo: Any Crew Injured/Killed: Items/Cash Stolen:
22	Area of the Ship being Attacked:
23	Last Observed Movements of Pirates/Suspect Craft:
24	Type of vessel (Whaler, Dhow, Fishing Vessel, Merchant Vessel)
25	Description of vessel (Colour, Name, Distinguishing Features)
26	Course and Speed of vessel when sighted

Details of Raiding Party

27	Number of Pirates/Robbers:
28	Dress/Physical Appearance:
29	Language Spoken:
30	Weapons Used:
31	Distinctive Details:
32	Craft Used:
33	Method of Approach:
34	Duration of Attack:
35	Aggressive/Violent:

Further Details

36	Action Taken by Master and Crew and its effectiveness:
37	Was Incident Reported to the Coastal Authority? If so to whom?
38	Preferred Communications with Reporting Ship: Appropriate Coast Radio Station/HF/MF/VHF/INMARSAT IDS (Plus Ocean Region Code)/MMSI
39	Action Taken by the Authorities:
40	Number of Crew/Nationality:
41	Please Attach with this Report – A Brief Description/Full Report/Master – Crew Statement of the Attack/Photographs taken if any.
42	Details of Self Protection Measures.

MSCHOA Vessel Movement Registration Form

The form 'Register a Vessel's Movements' is reproduced below from the MSCHOA website. The following is to be noted:

- The MSCHOA website should always be consulted to ensure that the most up to date version of the form is being used.
- Registration is required within the area bounded by 78°E, 10°S, 23°N and Suez.
- The form may be completed online by ship operators, (or Masters where vessels have internet access), but note that registration with the MSCHOA website is required before the form can be completed.
- MSCHOA will also accept faxed forms, and forms by email. Again ship operators should ensure that they and/or their vessels are in receipt of the latest version of the form.
- All fields with an asterisk (*) are obligatory.

Vessel's Details

Ship Name *	Flag State *
IMO Number *	MMSI Number *
Call Sign *	Ship's Master
Primary E-Mail *	Secondary E-Mail
Ship contact number *	Ship contact E-Mail *

Owner name	Operator name
Operator address	Operator telephone
Operator E-Mail	DPA name
DPA telephone	DPA E-Mail

Movement Details

Entry Point to High Risk Area * (78°E/10°S/23°N/Suez/Port)	Entry Date/Time to High Risk Area * (DD/MM/YYYY) (HH) (MM)
Exit Point from High Risk Area * (78°E/10°S/23°N/Suez/Port)	Entry Date/Time to High Risk Area * (DD/MM/YYYY) (HH) (MM)
Do you intend to transit the IRTC?	
*ETA to IRTC (times are in UTC/ Zulu time) * *	*(Tick box if applicable)*
*Direction * (East/West)*	
Do you intend to join a group transit?	Do you intend to join a National Convoy?
	*Which National Convoy are you joining? * (Chinese, Indian, Japanese, Korean, Russian, Turkish)*
Crew numbers and nationalities	Draught
Freeboard of lowest accessible deck in Metres(M) *	Planned Transit Speed *

Vessels Maximum Speed *	Cargo *(Crude Oil/Clean Oil/Arms/ Chemicals/ Gas/Passengers/Bulk Cargo/ Containers/Fishing/Ballast/ Others … Please Specify)*
	Hazardous cargo
Next Port of Call	Last Port of Call

Note: a. Items in italics only appear upon selection of prior options
b. Items in square brackets are options in a drop-down list

Movement Details

AIS to be left on through GOA?	AIS to be left on through HOA?
Anti-piracy measures in place?	
Crew Briefing	*Extra Lookouts*
Fire Hoses Rigged	*Fire Pump Ready*
Barbed/Razor Wire	Locked Doors
External Communication Plan	*Outboard Ladders Stowed*
Citadel	*Dummies Posted*
Night Vision Optics	*Manned Engine Room*
CCTV	*Crew Drills Completed*
Unarmed Security Team onboard	*Armed Security Team onboard*
Helicopter winch area?	*Doctor onboard?*
Helicopter landing area?	*Weapons held onboard?*
Additional Measures	*Any other information which may assist counter-piracy?*

Note: Items in italics appear when the 'Anti-piracy measure in place' option is selected.

Additional Guidance for Vessels Engaged in Fishing

The following guidance for vessels engaged in fishing has been provided by the following national fishing industry associations:

OPAGAC – Organizacion de Productores Asociados de Grandes Atuneros Congeladores

ANABAC – Asociacion Nacional de Armadores de Buques Atuneros Congeladores

ADDITIONAL GUIDANCE FOR VESSELS ENGAGED IN FISHING, IN THE GULF OF ADEN AND OFF THE COAST OF SOMALIA

I. RECOMMENDATIONS TO VESSELS IN FISHING ZONES

1. Non-Somali fishing vessels should avoid operating or transiting within 200 nm of the coast of Somalia, irrespective of whether or not they have been issued with licences to do so.

2. Do not start fishing operations when the radar indicates the presence of unidentified boats.

3. If polyester skiffs of a type typically used by pirates are sighted, move away from them at full speed, sailing into the wind and sea to make their navigation more difficult.

4. Avoid stopping at night, be alert and maintain bridge, deck and engine-room watch.

5. During fishing operations, when the vessel is more vulnerable, be alert and maintain radar watch in order to give maximum notice to the Authorities if an attack is in progress.

6. While navigating at night, use only the mandatory navigation and safety lights so as to prevent the glow of lighting attracting pirates, who sometimes are in boats without radar and are just lurking around.

7. While the vessel is drifting while fishing at night, keep guard at the bridge on deck and in the engine-room. Use only mandatory navigation and safety lights.

8. The engine must be ready for an immediate start-up.

9. Keep away from unidentified ships.

10. Use VHF as little as possible to avoid being heard by pirates and to make location more difficult.

11. Activate the AIS when maritime patrol aircraft are operating in the area to facilitate identification and tracking.

II. IDENTIFICATION

1. Managers are strongly recommended to register their fishing vessels with MSCHOA for the whole period of activity off the coast of Somalia. This should include communicating a full list of the crewmen on board and their vessels' intentions, if possible.

2. Carry out training prior to passage or fishing operations in the area.

3. Whenever fishing vessels are equipped with VMS devices, their manager should provide MSCHOA with access to VMS data.

4. Fishing vessels should avoid sailing through areas where they have been informed that suspected pirate 'Motherships' have been identified and should use all means to detect, as soon as

possible, any movement of large or small vessels that could be suspicious.

5. Fishing vessels should always identify themselves upon request from aircraft or ships from Operation ATALANTA or other international or national anti-piracy operation.

6. Military, merchant and fishing vessels should respond without delay to any identification request made by a fishing vessel being approached (to facilitate early action to make escape possible, especially if the vessel is fishing).

III. IN CASE OF ATTACK

1. In case of an attack or sighting a suspicious craft, warn the Authorities (UKMTO and MSCHOA) and the rest of the fleet.

2. Communicate the contact details of the second Master of the vessel (who is on land) whose knowledge of the vessel could contribute to the success of a military intervention.

Recommendations only for Purse Seiners

3. Evacuate all personnel from the deck and the crow's nest.

4. If pirates have taken control of the vessel and the purse seine is spread out, encourage the pirates to allow the nets to be recovered. If recovery of the purse seine is allowed, follow the instructions for its stowage and explain the functioning of the gear to avoid misunderstanding.

ANNEX G

Additional Advice for Leisure Craft Including Yachts

In view of the escalation in pirate attacks in the High Risk Area, the advice is NOT to enter this area.

However a yacht/leisure craft which, despite this advice, decides on such a passage is recommended to make contact in advance with the Naval/Military authorities.

See the MSCHOA (www.MSCHOA.com) and ISAF (International Sailing Federation) websites for the most up to date information on this process. There is also information on the NATO Shipping Centre website (www.shipping.nato.int.)

ISAF Cruising microsite - www.sailing.org/cruising.

Supporting Organisations

<u>**i. BMP4 Signatories**</u>

BIMCO

BIMCO is an independent international shipping association, with a membership composed of ship owners, managers, brokers, agents and many other stakeholders with vested interests in the shipping industry. The association acts on behalf of its global membership to promote higher standards and greater harmony in regulatory matters. It is a catalyst for the development and promotion of fair and equitable international shipping policy BIMCO is accredited as a Non-Governmental Organisation (NGO) holds observer status with a number of United Nations organs and is in close dialogue with maritime administrations regulatory institutions and other stakeholders within the EU the USA and Asia. The association provides one of the most comprehensive sources of practical shipping information and a broad range of advisory and consulting services to its members. www.bimco.org

Cruise Lines International Association

Cruise Lines International Association (CLIA) is the world's largest cruise association and is comprised of 25 of the world's major cruise lines. CLIA participates in the international regulatory and policy development process and promotes all measures that foster a safe, secure and healthy cruise ship environment. CLIA actively monitors international shipping policy and develops recommendations to its membership. CLIA serves as a non-governmental consultative organization to the International Maritime Organization. www.cruising.org

 **International Chamber of Shipping**

The International Chamber of Shipping (ICS) is the international trade association for merchant ship operators. ICS represents the collective views of the international industry from different nations, sectors and trades. ICS membership comprises national shipowners' associations representing over 75% of the world's merchant fleet. A major focus of ICS activity is the International Maritime Organization (IMO) the United Nations agency with responsibility for the safety of life at sea and the protection of the marine environment. ICS is heavily involved in a wide variety of areas including any technical, legal and operational matters affecting merchant ships. ICS is unique in that it represents the global interests of all the different trades in the industry: bulk carrier operators, tanker operators, passenger ship operators and container liner trades, including shipowners and third party ship managers. www.marisec.org

 IGP&I. (The International Group of P&I Clubs)

The thirteen principal underwriting member clubs of the **International Group of P&I Clubs** ('the Group') between them provide liability cover (protection and indemnity) for approximately 90% of the world's ocean-going tonnage. Each Group club is an independent, non-profit making mutual insurance association, providing cover for its ship-owner and charterer members against third party liabilities relating to the use and operation of ships. Each club is controlled by its members through a board of directors or committee elected from the membership Clubs cover a wide range of liabilities including personal injury to crew, passengers and others on board, cargo loss and damage, oil pollution, wreck removal and dock damage. Clubs also provide a wide range of services to their members on claims, legal issues and loss prevention, and often play a leading role in the management of casualties. www.igpandi.org

ICC International Maritime Bureau

IMB

The main objective of the International Maritime Bureau's Piracy Reporting Centre (PRC) is to be the first point of contact for the shipmaster to report an actual or attempted attack or even suspicious movements thus initiating the process of response. The PRC raises awareness within the shipping industry, which includes the shipmaster, ship-owner, insurance companies, traders, etc, of the areas of high risk associated with piratical attacks or specific ports and anchorages associated with armed robberies on board ships. They work closely with various governments and law enforcement agencies, and are involved in information sharing in an attempt to reduce and ultimately eradicate piracy. www.icc-ccs.org/piracy-reporting-centre

IMEC International Maritime Employers' Committee Ltd (IMEC)

IMEC IMEC is the only international employers' organisation dedicated to maritime industrial relations, with offices in London and Manila, and a membership of over 140 of some of the world's largest ship owners and managers, covering some 7,500 ships and 185,000 seafarers. Many of these ships/seafarers are covered by IBF agreements, which IMEC, as a founder member of the Joint Negotiating Group, negotiates on behalf of the membership. IMEC also invests heavily in training, with, amongst other projects, Cadet programs being managed in-house for over 800 future Officers, who are provided free of charge to the membership. www.imec.org.uk

 **INTERCARGO**

INTERCARGO is the short name for the International Association of Dry Cargo Ship-owners. Since 1980, it has represented the interests of owners, operators and managers of dry cargo shipping and works closely with the other international associations to promote a safe, high quality, efficient and profitable industry. www.intercargo.org

 **InterManager**

InterManager is the international trade association for the shipmanagement industry. InterManager's members are in-house or third party ship managers, crew managers or related organisations or businesses from throughout the shipping industry. Collectively InterManager members are involved in the management of more than 4,370 ships and responsible for some 250,000 seafarers. InterManager is the only organisation exclusively dedicated to representing the shipmanagement industry. It is a recognised and well-respected organisation which represents its members at international level, lobbying on their behalf to ensure their views and needs are taken into account within the world-wide maritime industry. InterManager is committed to improving transparency and governance in the shipping world and ensuring high standards are maintained throughout the shipmanagement sector. www.intermanager.org

INTERTANKO

INTERTANKO is the International Association of Independent Tanker Owners INTERTANKO has been the voice of independent tanker owners since 1970, ensuring that the oil that keeps the world turning is shipped safely, responsibly and competitively. Membership is open to independent tanker owners and operators of oil and chemical tankers, i.e. non-oil companies and non-state controlled tanker owners, who fulfil the Association's membership criteria. Independent owners operate some 75% of the world's tanker fleet and the vast majority are INTERTANKO members. As of January 2011, the organisation had 250 members, whose combined fleet comprises some 3,050 tankers totalling 285 million dwt. INTERTANKO's associate membership stands at some 320 companies with an interest in shipping of oil and chemicals. www.intertanko.com

 INTERNATIONAL SHIPPING FEDERATION

The International Shipping Federation (ISF) is the principal international employers' organisation for the shipping industry, representing all sectors and trades. ISF membership comprises national shipowners' associations whose member shipping companies together operate 75% of the world's merchant tonnage and employ a commensurate proportion of the world's 1.25 million seafarers. Established in 1909, ISF is concerned with all labour affairs, manpower and training, and seafarers' health and welfare issues that may have an impact on international shipping. www.marisec.org

ITF (International Transport Workers Federation)

ITF (International Transport Workers Federation) The International Transport Workers' Federation (ITF) is an international trade union federation of transport workers' unions. Any independent trade union with members in the transport industry is eligible for membership of the ITF. The ITF has been helping seafarers since 1896 and today represents the interests of seafarers worldwide, of whom over 600,000 are members of ITF affiliated unions. The ITF is working to improve conditions for seafarers of all nationalities and to ensure adequate regulation of the shipping industry to protect the interests and rights of the workers. The ITF helps crews regardless of their nationality or the flag of their ship. www.itfseafarers.org www.itfglobal.org

 The International Parcel Tankers Association

The International Parcel Tankers Association was formed in 1987 to represent the interests of the specialised chemical/parcel tanker fleet and has since developed into an established representative body for ship owners operating IMO classified chemical/parcel tankers, being recognised as a focal point through which regulatory authorities and trade organisations may liaise with such owners. IPTA was granted consultative status as a Non-Governmental Organisation to the International Maritime Organization (IMO) in 1997 and is wholly supportive of the IMO as the only body to introduce and monitor compliance with international maritime legislation. www.ipta.org.uk

 **JHC (Joint Hull Committee)**

The Joint Hull Committee (JHC) was founded in 1910 and comprises underwriting representatives from both Lloyd's syndicates and the IUA company market. It discusses all matters connected with hull insurance, and represents the interests of those writing marine hull business within the London market. It liaises widely with the broad maritime sector. The JHC, from time to time, issues circulars to the market which are of relevance to the hull underwriting community and these may include new model wordings, information about developments in shipping, and notices of briefings.

Joint War Committee   JWC (Joint War Committee)

The Joint War Committee (JWC) comprises underwriting representatives from both Lloyd's syndicates and the IUA company market. It discusses all matters connected with hull war insurance, and represents the interests of those writing marine hull war business within the London market. JWC takes advice from independent security advisers and from time to time, issues updates to its published Listed Areas. These are the areas of perceived enhanced risk for those writing the range of perils insured in the war market where coverage may be arranged against the risks of confiscation, derelict weapons, piracy, strikes, terrorism and war.

Oil Companies International Marine Forum (OCIMF)

The Oil Companies International Marine Forum (OCIMF) is a voluntary association of oil companies having an interest in the shipment and terminalling of crude oil and oil products. Our mission is to be the foremost authority on the safe and environmentally responsible operation of oil tankers, terminals and offshore support vessels, promoting continuous improvement in standards of design and operation. www.ocimf.org

SIGTTO SIGTTO

(The Society of International Gas Tanker and Terminal Operators) was established in 1979 to encourage safe and responsible operation of liquefied gas tankers and marine terminals handling liquefied gas, to develop advice and guidance for best industry practice among its members and to promote criteria for best practice to all who either have responsibilities for, or an interest in, the continuing safety of gas tankers and terminals. The Society is registered as a 'not for profit' entity in Bermuda and is owned by its members who are predominately the owners of assets in the LPG/LNG ship and terminal business. The Society has observer status at the IMO. www.sigtto.org

The Mission to Seafarers

Caring for seafarers
around the world

The Mission to Seafarers offers emergency assistance, practical support, and a friendly welcome to crews visiting 230 ports around the world. Whether caring for victims of piracy or providing a lifeline to those stranded in foreign ports, we are there for the globe's 1.2 million merchant seafarers of all ranks, nationalities and beliefs. www.missiontoseafarers.org

 The World Shipping Council (WSC)

WORLD SHIPPING COUNCIL
PARTNERS IN TRADE

The World Shipping Council (WSC)) is the trade association that represents the international liner shipping industry. WSC's member lines operate containerships, roll-on/roll-off, and car carrier vessels that account for approximately 90 percent of the global liner vessel capacity. Collectively, these services transport about 60 percent of the value of global seaborne trade, or more than US$ 4 trillion worth of goods annually. The World Shipping Council's goal is to provide a coordinated voice for the liner shipping industry in its work with policymakers and other industry groups to develop actionable solutions for some of the world's most challenging transportation problems. WSC serves as a non-governmental organization at the International Maritime Organization (IMO). www.worldshipping.org

ii. Naval/Military Forces/Law Enforcement Organisations supporting BMP4

 Combined Maritime Forces (CMF)

Combined Maritime Forces is a 25 nation coalition committed to ensuring regional security. CMF operates in accordance with international law and relevant United Nations Security Council Resolutions and is supported by three distinct missions. Combined Task Force (CTF) 150 operates in the Red Sea, Gulf of Aden, Indian Ocean, Arabian Sea and the Gulf of Oman conducting Maritime Security Operations. CTF 151 operates in the Gulf of Aden and Somali Basin and the Indian Ocean to deter, disrupt and suppress piracy, protecting the safe passage of maritime vessels of any nationality. CTF 152 operates in the Arabian Gulf conducting maritime security operations in conjunction with Gulf Cooperation Council (GCC) partners in order to prevent destabilizing activities. www.cusnc.navy.mil/cmf/cmf_command.html

 EU NAVFOR (The European Union Naval Force)

EUNAVFOR is the main coordinating authority which operates the Maritime Security Centre (Horn of Africa). Operation Atalanta includes the deployment of a major EU Naval Task Group into the region to improve maritime security off the Somali coast. Additionally the mission also encompasses a broad range of liaison, both regionally and with industry, to help establish best practices and to disseminate information through its 24/7 manned Maritime Security Centre-Horn of Africa (MSC-HOA) and through the website www.mschoa.org

INTERPOL

INTERPOL is the world's largest international police organization, with 188 member countries. Created in 1923, it facilitates cross-border police co-operation, and supports and assists all organizations, authorities and services whose mission is to prevent or combat international crime.

INTERPOL's Maritime task Force (MPTF) was set up in January 2010 to co-ordinate the Organization's international response to the maritime piracy threat in its various facets by:

- Improving the global collection, preservation, analysis and dissemination of piracy-related evidence and intelligence in aid of criminal investigations and prosecutions by its member countries; and
- Developing police and judicial investigative and prosecution capabilities in Eastern Africa in partnership with key international actors and donors.

www.interpol.int

MARLO The U.S. Navy Maritime Liaison Office

The Maritime Liaison Office (MARLO) mission is to facilitate the exchange of information between the United States Navy, Combined Maritime Forces, and the commercial maritime community in the United States Central Command's (CENTCOM) Area of Responsibility. MARLO operates as a conduit for information focused on the safety and security of shipping and is committed to assisting all members of the commercial maritime community. To help combat piracy, MARLO serves as a secondary emergency point of contact for mariners in distress (after UKMTO) and also disseminates transit guidance to the maritime industry. MARLO disseminates guidance to merchant shippers via briefings, website, email, and duty phone concerning Naval Exercises, Boardings, Aids to Navigation, Environmental Issues, MEDEVAC Assistance, Security and Augments, Regional Search and Rescue Centres.

 Maritime Security Centre Horn of Africa (MSCHOA)

The Maritime Security Centre – Horn of Africa (MSCHOA) aims to provide a service to mariners in the Gulf of Aden, the Somali Basin and off the Horn of Africa. It is a Coordination Centre dedicated to safeguarding legitimate freedom of navigation in the light of increasing risks of pirate attack against merchant shipping in the region, in support of the UN Security Council's Resolutions (UNSCR) 1814, 1816 and 1838. Through close dialogue with shipping companies, masters and other interested parties, MSCHOA will build up a picture of vulnerable shipping in these waters and their approaches. The Centre, which is manned by military and merchant navy personnel from several countries, will then coordinate with a range of military forces operating in the region to provide support and protection to mariners. There is a clear need to protect ships and their crews from illegitimate and dangerous attacks, safeguarding a key global trade route. www.mschoa.org

NATO Shipping Centre (NSC)

NATO Shipping Centre (NSC) provides the commercial link with NATO's Maritime Forces. The NSC is NATO's primary point of contact with the maritime community and is used by NATO as the tool for communicating and coordinating initiatives and efforts with other military actors (most notably UK MTO, MSCHOA and MARLO) as well as directly with the maritime community, and thereby supporting the overall efforts to reduce the incidence of piracy. www.shipping.nato.int

 Operation Ocean Shield

Operation Ocean Shield is NATO's contribution to international efforts to combat piracy off the Horn of Africa. The operation develops a distinctive NATO role based on the broad strength of the Alliance by adopting a more comprehensive approach to counter-piracy efforts. NATO's counter piracy efforts focus on at-sea counter-piracy operations, support to the maritime community to take actions to reduce incidence of piracy, as well as regional-state counter-piracy capacity building. The operation is designed to complement the efforts of existing international organisations and forces operating in the area.

 **UKMTO**

The UK Maritime Trade Operations (UKMTO) office in Dubai acts as the primary point of contact for merchant vessels and liaison with military forces in the region. UKMTO also administers the Voluntary Reporting Scheme, under which merchant vessels are encouraged to send regular reports, providing their position/course/ speed and ETA at their next port while transiting the region bound by Suez, 78°E and 10°S. UKMTO subsequently tracks vessels and the positional information is passed to CMF and EU headquarters. Emerging and relevant information affecting commercial traffic can then be passed directly to ships, rather than by company offices, improving responsiveness to any incident and saving time. For further information or to join the Voluntary Reporting Scheme, please contact UKMTO or MSCHOA Email: ukmto@eim.ae

NOT TO BE USED FOR NAVIGATION

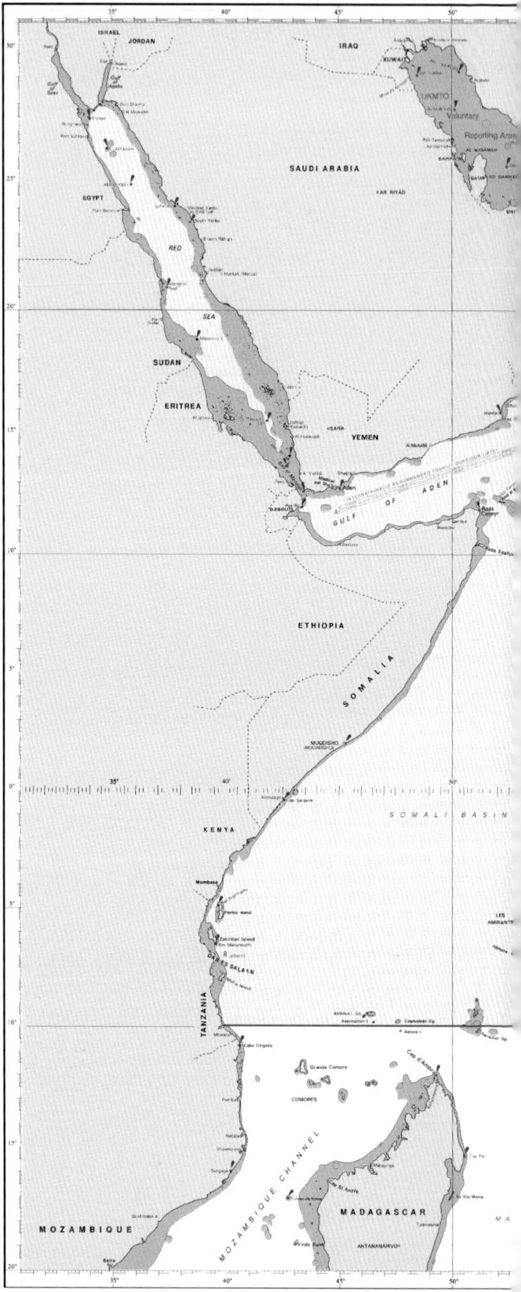

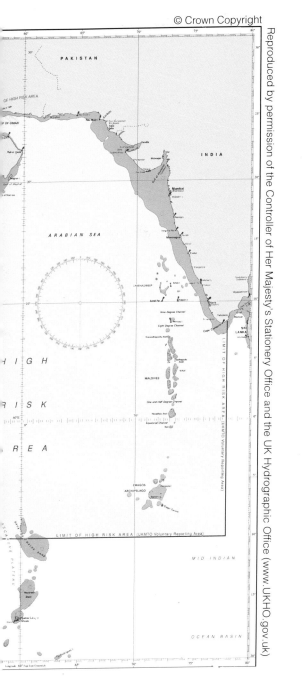